My First NFL Book

CHICAGO BEARS

Amy Sawyer

LET'S READ
AV²
BY WEIGL™
ADDED VALUE • AUDIO VISUAL

Go to **www.av2books.com**, and enter this book's unique code.

BOOK CODE

D 5 8 8 8 6 6

AV² by Weigl brings you media enhanced books that support active learning.

AV² provides enriched content that supplements and complements this book. Weigl's AV² books strive to create inspired learning and engage young minds in a total learning experience.

Your AV² Media Enhanced books come alive with...

Audio
Listen to sections of the book read aloud.

Video
Watch informative video clips.

Embedded Weblinks
Gain additional information for research.

Try This!
Complete activities and hands-on experiments.

Key Words
Study vocabulary, and complete a matching word activity.

Quizzes
Test your knowledge.

Slide Show
View images and captions, and prepare a presentation.

... and much, much more!

Published by AV² by Weigl
350 5ᵗʰ Avenue, 59ᵗʰ Floor
New York, NY 10118

Website: www.av2books.com

Printed in the United States of America in Brainerd, Minnesota
1 2 3 4 5 6 7 8 9 0 21 20 19 18 17

032017
020317

Editor: Katie Gillespie
Art Director: Terry Paulhus

Weigl acknowledges Getty Images as the primary image supplier for this title.

Library of Congress Control Number: 2017930538

ISBN 978-1-4896-5490-8 (hardcover)
ISBN 978-1-4896-5492-2 (multi-user eBook)

My First NFL Book

CHICAGO BEARS

CONTENTS

Team History

The Bears were one of the first teams in the NFL. They started playing in a small town in Illinois in 1920. The team moved to Chicago one year later. George Halas was their first coach. He helped to start both the Bears and the NFL.

Bears player Harold "Red" Grange was one of the first 17 people in the Pro Football Hall of Fame.

The Stadium

Soldier Field is home to the Bears. It is the second smallest stadium in the NFL. Its name honors soldiers in the United States military. The stadium opened in 1924. New sections were added in 2003.

Soldier Field is in Chicago, Illinois, on the shore of Lake Michigan.

Team Spirit

Staley Da Bear is the team's mascot. He wears the number 00. He was named after the company that started the team. It was called A. E. Staley.

Staley gives fans and players high fives.

The Jerseys

The Bears' team colors are navy blue, orange, and white. The colors were picked to match the University of Illinois' colors. The left sleeve has the letters "GSH" on it. This stands for former coach and owner George S. Halas.

The Helmet

The players wear blue helmets with the team logo on each side. The "C" was added to the helmets in 1962. The logo used to be all white. It is now orange with white around it.

The last time a member of the Bears played without a helmet was 1940.

13

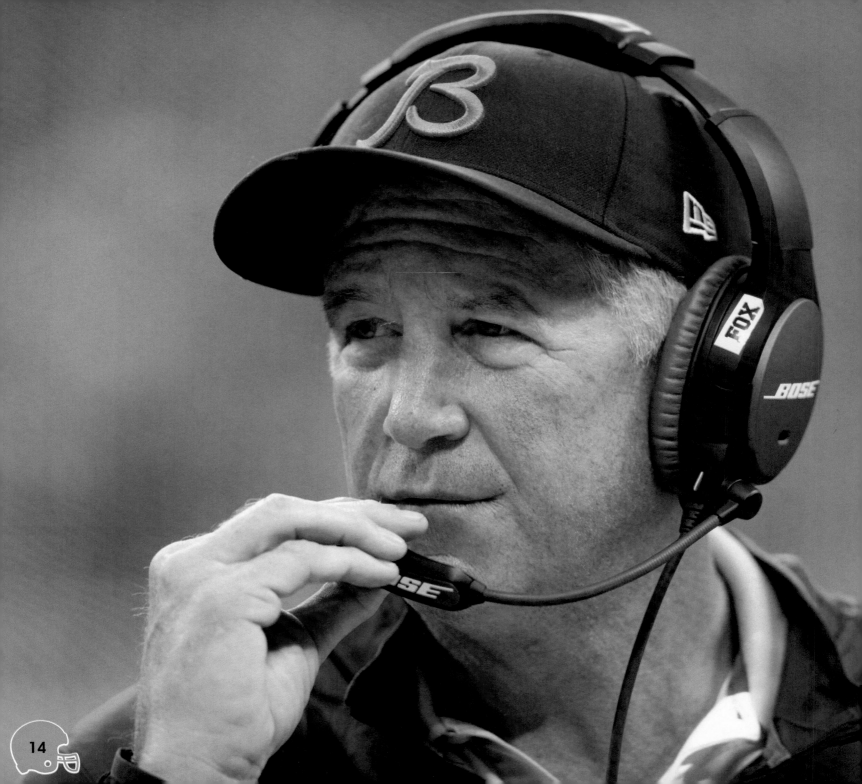

The Coach

John Fox was named head coach of the Bears in 2015. Part of his job is to help players use their skills. Fox has been a head coach in the NFL since 2002. He led two of his former teams to the Super Bowl.

Player Positions

Football teams have an offense and a defense. The quarterback calls the plays for the offense. The defense stops the other team from scoring. Special teams are brought onto the field when the ball is going to be kicked.

It is against the rules to tackle a kicker or punter during a kick.

Kyle Long plays offense. He helps protect the quarterback. Long was the Bears' first draft pick in 2013. He was named to the Pro Bowl in his first three seasons. No other Bears lineman has done that. Coaches, players, and fans pick the best players to play in the Pro Bowl each year.

Walter Payton was a running back for the Bears from 1975 to 1987. He scored 125 touchdowns. That is the second most touchdowns ever scored in the NFL. When he retired, Payton held 10 NFL records. He also held 24 Bears records. He is in the Pro Football Hall of Fame.

Famous Player

Team Records

The Bears have nine league championships. That is the second most in the NFL. The Bears have had many great players. Robbie Gould is one. He is their all-time leading scorer, with 1,207 points. Devin Hester is another great player. He holds five team records, including most kickoff returns.

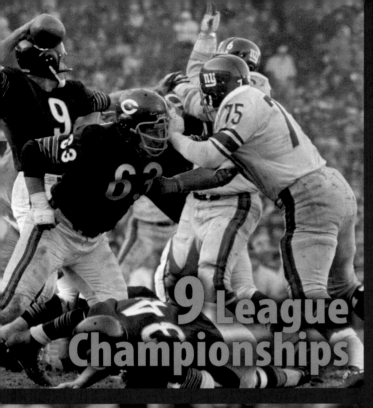

9 League Championships

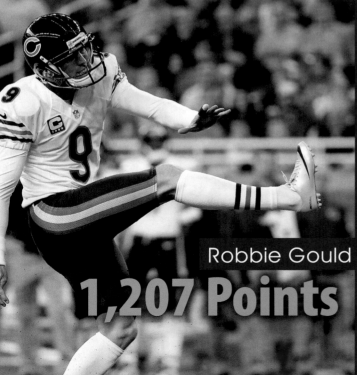

Robbie Gould

1,207 Points

Devin Hester

5 Team Records

By the Numbers

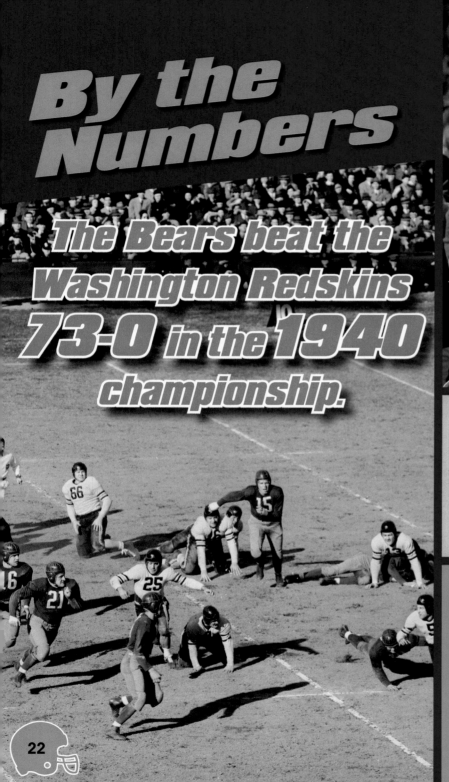

The Bears beat the Washington Redskins **73-0** in the **1940** championship.

The Bears average **61,387 attendees** per home game.

The Bears **won 17 straight games** from 1933 to 1934.

14 player numbers have been retired.

Soldier Field cost **$13 million** to build.

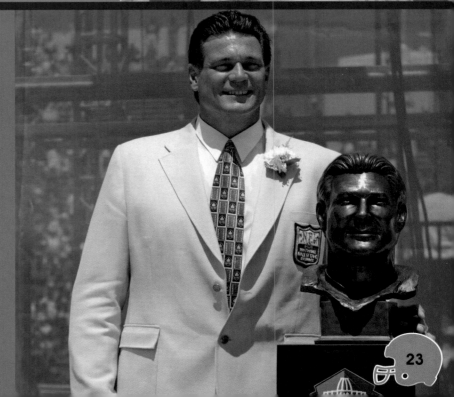

27

Chicago Bears are in the **Pro Football Hall of Fame**. This is more than any other NFL team.

Quiz

1. When were new sections added to Soldier Field?

2. What number does Staley wear?

3. What does "GSH" stand for?

4. Who is the Bears' all-time leading scorer?

5. How many Bears player numbers have been retired?

ANSWERS 1. 2003 2. 00 3. George S. Halas 4. Robbie Gould 5. 14

24